Games and Puzzles

Grade K

Copyright © 2011 Popular Book Company (Canada) Limited

Printed in China

ISBN: 978-1-897457-86-3

Contents

Games and Puzzles

Kindergarten

English

Math

ISBN: 978-1-897457-86-3

English

A

B

C

D

E

ISBN: 978-1-897457-86-3

Look at the things that begin with the sound of b. Find and colour the words in the word search.

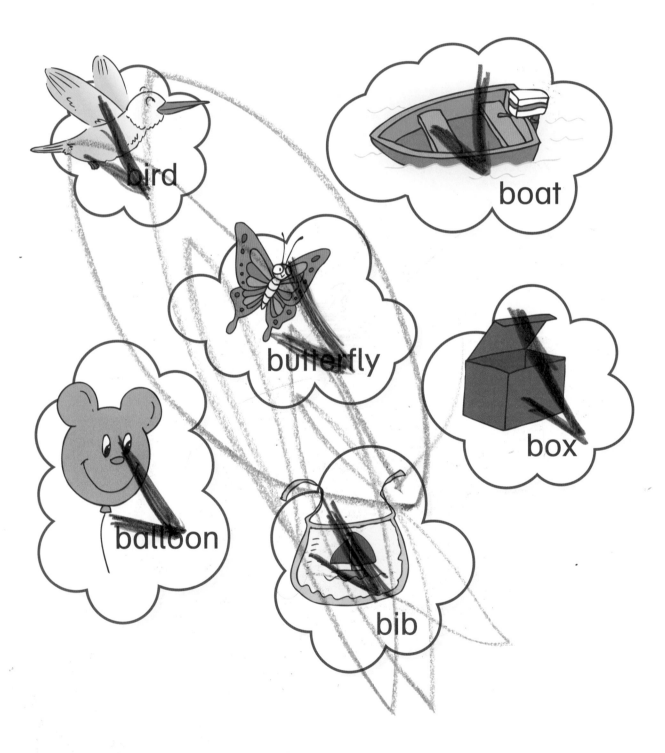

b_ke

_at

t	y	z	b	o	a	t	e
k	h	w	u	d	j	l	v
u	b	a	t	n	b	q	f
g	v	f	t	h	m	z	w
b	i	k	e	b	l	p	x
h	b	i	r	d	c	n	j
q	i	c	f	t	g	b	s
j	b	a	l	l	o	o	n
b	v	m	y	p	t	x	i

ISBN: 978-1-897457-86-3

Look at the picture clues. Solve the crossword puzzle with the words that begin with the sound of **c** in the word bank.

candle

cake

cat

car

carrot

cap

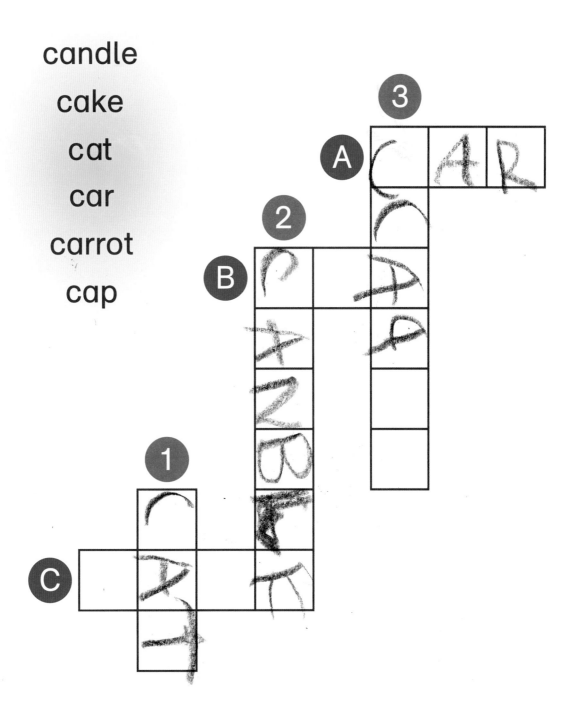

Didi the Dog is looking for a bone. Help him by colouring the path with things that begin with the sound of **d**.

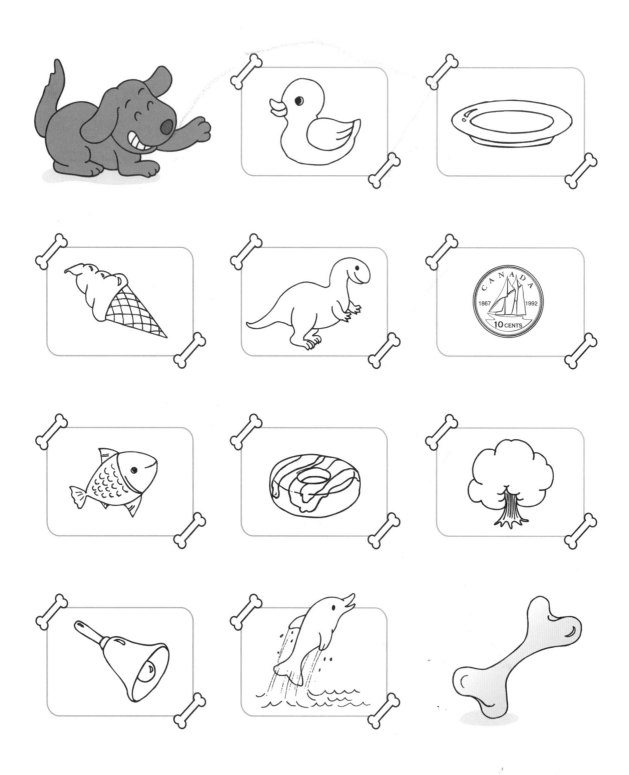

ISBN: 978-1-897457-86-3

Fanny the Fairy is learning to use her wand. She wants to make the things that begin with the sound of **f** disappear. Help her by crossing out **✗** these things.

Look for the names of things that begin with the sound of **g** in the word search. Colour the boxes.

ISBN: 978-1-897457-86-3

A	T	H	B	L	U	X
M	G	I	O	C	G	E
K	H	G	Z	G	U	N
G	O	O	S	E	I	V
U	S	A	H	L	T	J
M	T	T	P	F	A	D
W	N	D	G	I	R	L
P	Y	M	T	H	B	Q

ISBN: 978-1-897457-86-3

Daddy has got something on his head. Colour the spaces with things that begin with the sound of **h** to find out what it is.

ISBN: 978-1-897457-86-3

Jerry the Juggler is tossing some balls. Colour the balls with things that begin with the sound of j.

Little Koala wants to play with Little Kitten. Help her get to Little Kitten by colouring the things that begin with the sound of **k**.

ISBN: 978-1-897457-86-3

Lily the Ladybug wants to crawl down the leaf. Colour her path following the pictures of things that begin with the sound of l.

Milly cannot see the images of things that begin with the sound of **m** in the magic mirror. Draw the things in the mirror for her.

Moon   Mushroom   Mittens

ISBN: 978-1-897457-86-3

Nigel is putting things that begin with the sound of n into the net. Circle ○ the things and draw them in the net.

ISBN: 978-1-897457-86-3

Priscilla is looking at things that begin with the sound of **p**.
Help her complete their names in the boxes.

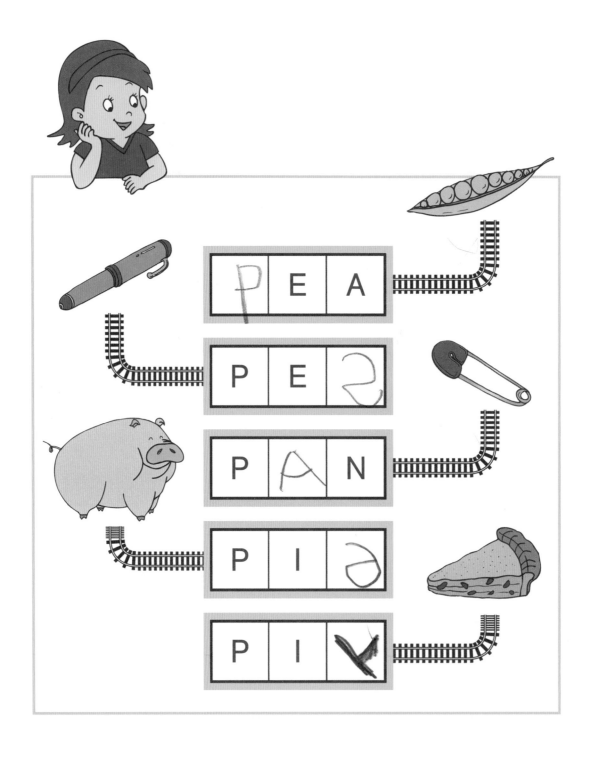

ISBN: 978-1-897457-86-3

Mommy is making a quilt. Colour the patches with things that begin with the sound of q.

Rupert the Rocket wants to stop on the R-planets. Colour the planets with things that begin with the sound of r.

ISBN: 978-1-897457-86-3

Look at the snake. Colour the patches with things that begin with the sound of s.

ISBN: 978-1-897457-86-3

Look at the picture clues. Solve the crossword puzzle with the words that begin with the sound of t in the word bank.

Across

A

B

C

Down

1

2

3

ISBN: 978-1-897457-86-3

A crossword puzzle:

```
        1
   A  [t][e][N][t]              3
                          B  [t][i][e]
                             [t][o][a]
              2
   C  [t][u][R][t][i][e]
      [h]       [u]
      [b]       [R]
      [R]       [k]
      [u]       [e]
      [z]       [K]
      [h]
```

Word list:
tie
turkey
toothbrush
turtle
tent
top

ISBN: 978-1-897457-86-3

Vivi the Vacuum Cleaner wants to suck up things that begin with the sound of **v**. Colour the things he wants to suck up.

ISBN: 978-1-897457-86-3

Winnie the Witch and Willie the Wizard are making some magic soup with things that begin with the sound of w. Colour the things.

Look at the cards. Decide whether the things begin with the sound of x or y. Circle ◯ the correct letters.

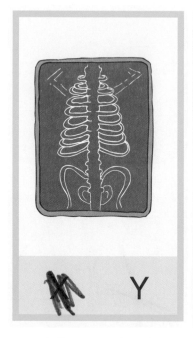

X   Y

X   Y

X   Y

X   Y

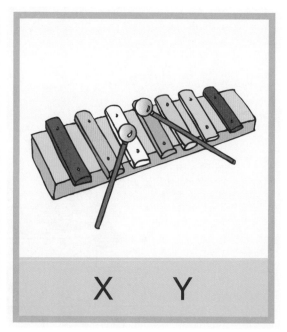

X   Y

ISBN: 978-1-897457-86-3

Draw lines to match the pictures with the words that begin with the sound of z. Colour the pictures.

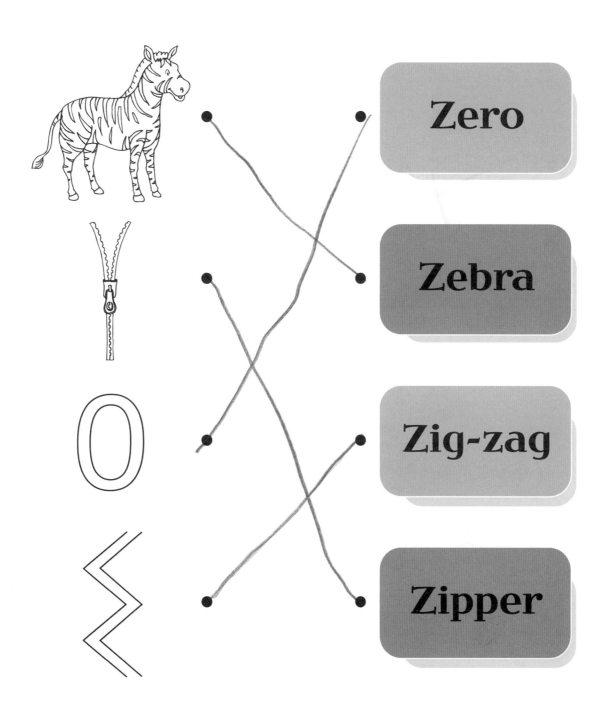

Zero

Zebra

Zig-zag

Zipper

ISBN: 978-1-897457-86-3

Little Alien is learning the names of things that end with the sound of **b**. Help him finish the word search by colouring the boxes with these words.

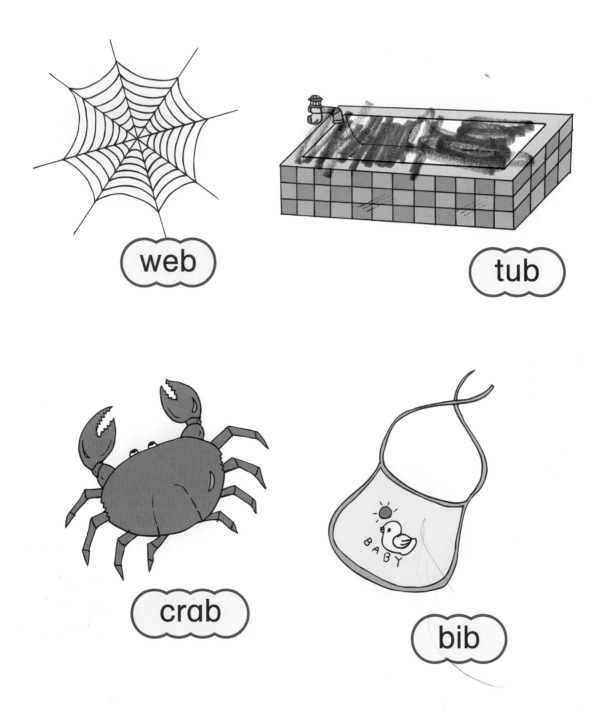

web

tub

crab

bib

ISBN: 978-1-897457-86-3

sub

globe

e	w	c	r	t	b	s	u
s	e	t	b	u	w	e	r
u	c	r	a	b	r	b	i
s	i	l	c	e	g	l	a
u	t	e	r	b	l	o	g
b	w	w	u	s	o	c	u
g	l	t	b	i	b	t	a
s	r	t	e	w	e	b	l

Thomas is looking at a big animal at the safari. Colour the spaces according to the ending sounds of the things.

d -   t -   s -

ISBN: 978-1-897457-86-3

Fill in the missing letters. Colour the patches with things that end with the sound of f.

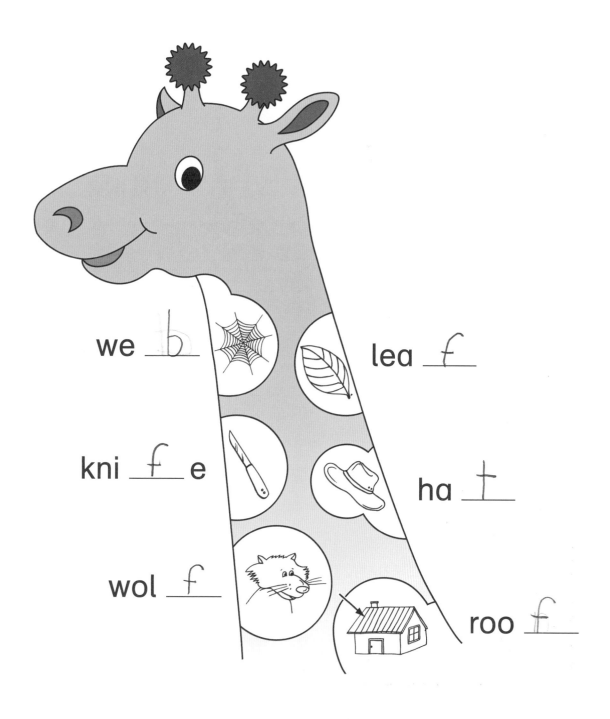

we __b__

lea __f__

kni __f__ e

ha __t__

wol __f__

roo __f__

ISBN: 978-1-897457-86-3

Look at the picture. Colour the things that end with the sound of **g** purple. Colour those that end with the sound of **k** pink.

ISBN: 978-1-897457-86-3

Circle ◯ the thing that ends with the sound of l in each row.

ISBN: 978-1-897457-86-3

Sam wants to play in the park. Help him by filling in the missing letter under each picture. Then colour his path following these words.

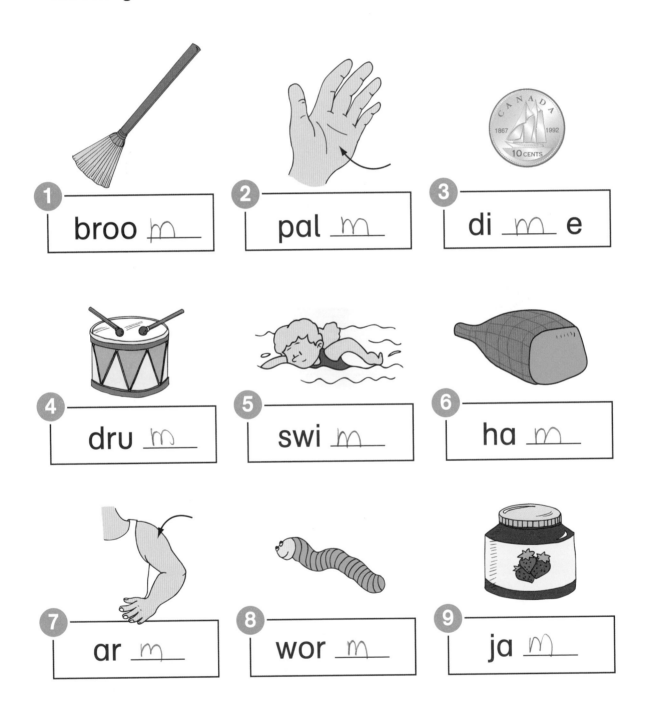

1 broo _m_

2 pal _m_

3 di _m_ e

4 dru _m_

5 swi _m_

6 ha _m_

7 ar _m_

8 wor _m_

9 ja _m_

ISBN: 978-1-897457-86-3

ISBN: 978-1-897457-86-3

Look at the picture clues. Solve the crossword puzzle and answer the question.

ISBN: 978-1-897457-86-3

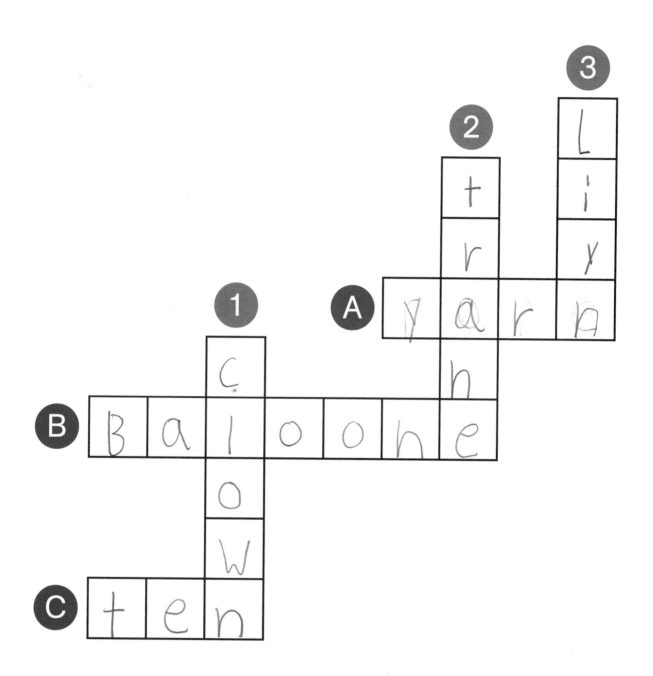

What is the ending sound of all these things?

enn

ISBN: 978-1-897457-86-3

English

Peter is looking for things that end with the sound of **p** in his room. Help him by circling ◯ these things.

ISBN: 978-1-897457-86-3

Barry the Big Bear wants to get to the jar of honey. Colour his path by following the things that end with the sound of r.

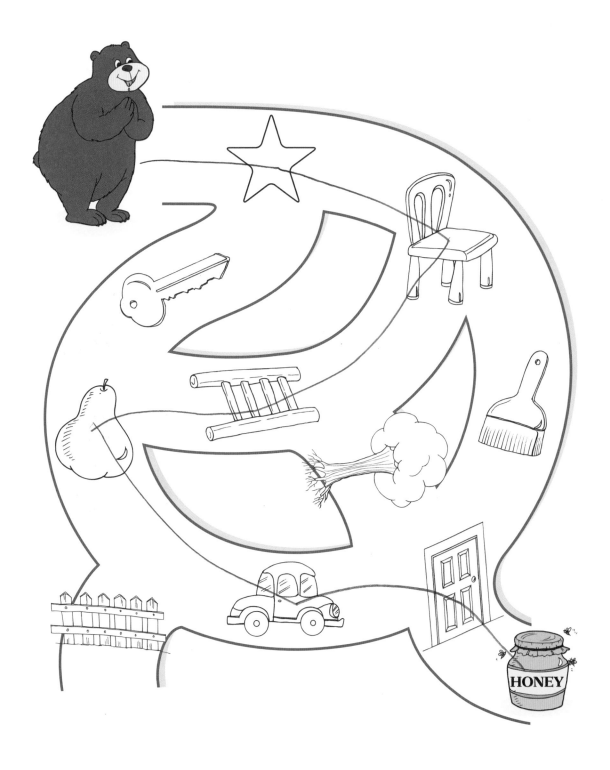

Draw lines to match the words that end with the sound of
v with the pictures.

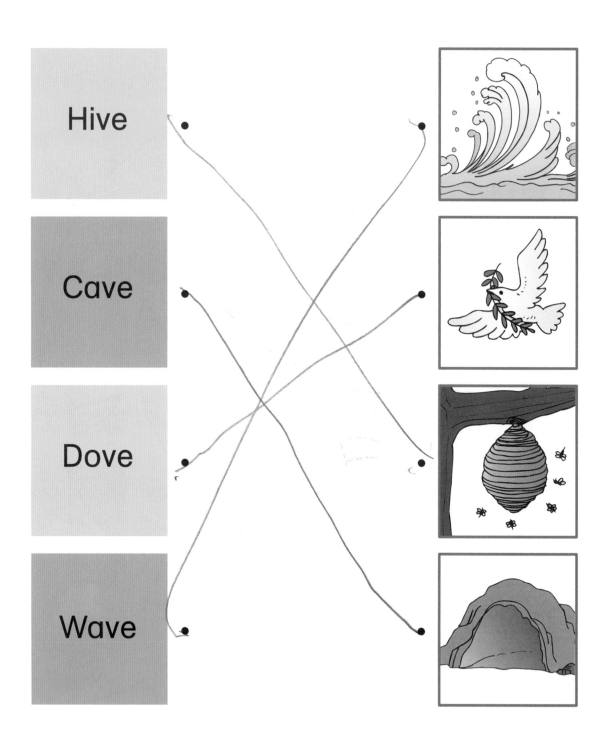

Hive

Cave

Dove

Wave

ISBN: 978-1-897457-86-3

Look at each row of cards. Colour the animal with the same beginning sound as the one on the left.

English

Benny is doing a worksheet. Help him by writing the beginning letter of each thing in the circle and the ending letter in the square.

ISBN: 978-1-897457-86-3

Math

ISBN: 978-1-897457-86-3

Four children are in the park. Count and write how many children are playing.

_____ children are playing.

ISBN: 978-1-897457-86-3

Bill has some goldfish. Count and write how many goldfish he has.

Bill has _____ goldfish.

ISBN: 978-1-897457-86-3

Math

Lisa has balls of different patterns. Which two patterns are the same in number? Colour them.

ISBN: 978-1-897457-86-3

Bill is drawing on his computer. Count and circle the correct numbers.

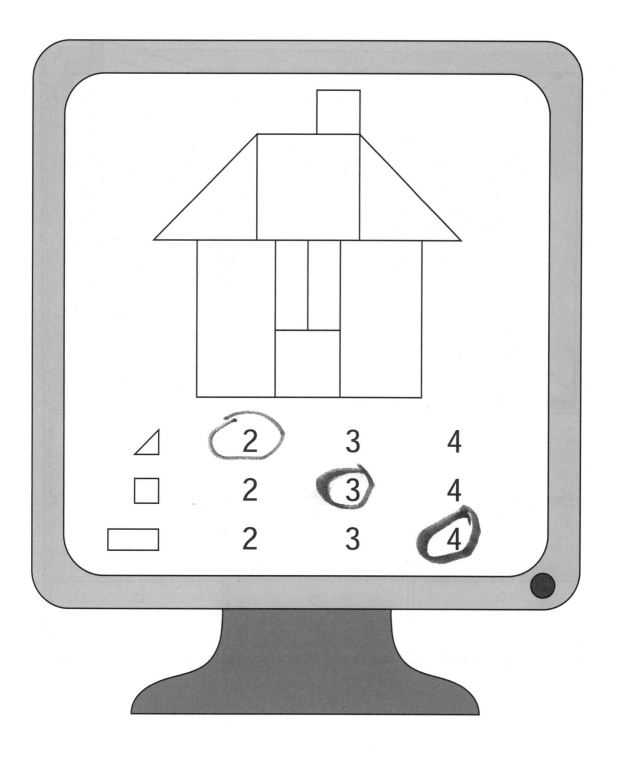

Mike has **4** caps in his wardrobe. Draw the missing caps.

ISBN: 978-1-897457-86-3

Shirley and Daisy have saved some coins. Count and circle the correct answer.

Who has more coins?

ISBN: 978-1-897457-86-3

Paul has put his presents under the Christmas tree. Count and write how many presents he has got.

Paul has got _____5_____ presents.

ISBN: 978-1-897457-86-3

Ada is 5 years old. Draw **5** candles on her birthday cake.
Colour the cake.

ISBN: 978-1-897457-86-3

There are many kites in the sky. Count and circle the correct answers.

ISBN: 978-1-897457-86-3

 is the most in number.

ISBN: 978-1-897457-86-3

Alan has drawn a train with shapes. Count and circle the correct numbers. Colour the train.

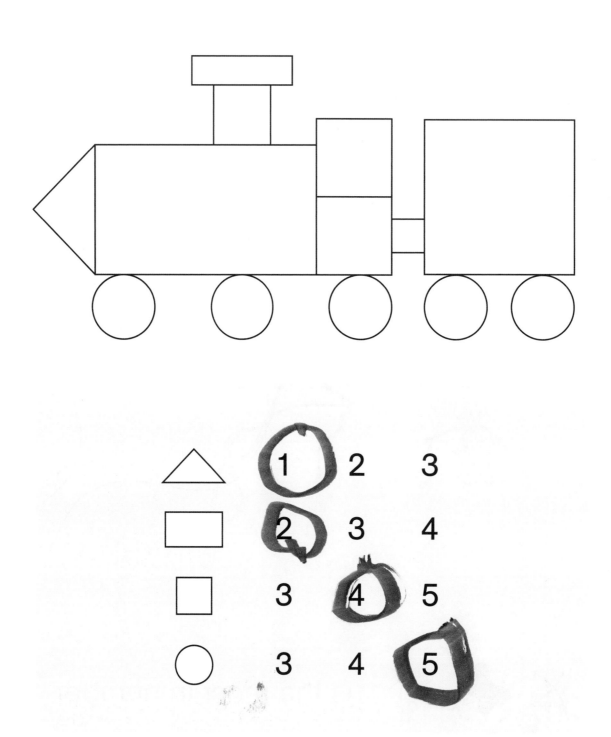

Mary is watching cartoons on the couch. How long is the couch? Count the  and write the correct number.

The couch is about _____ 8 long.

Eric has **6** Easter eggs. Draw the missing eggs in the basket. Colour the eggs.

ISBN: 978-1-897457-86-3

How many fruits did Mom buy? Count and draw lines to match.

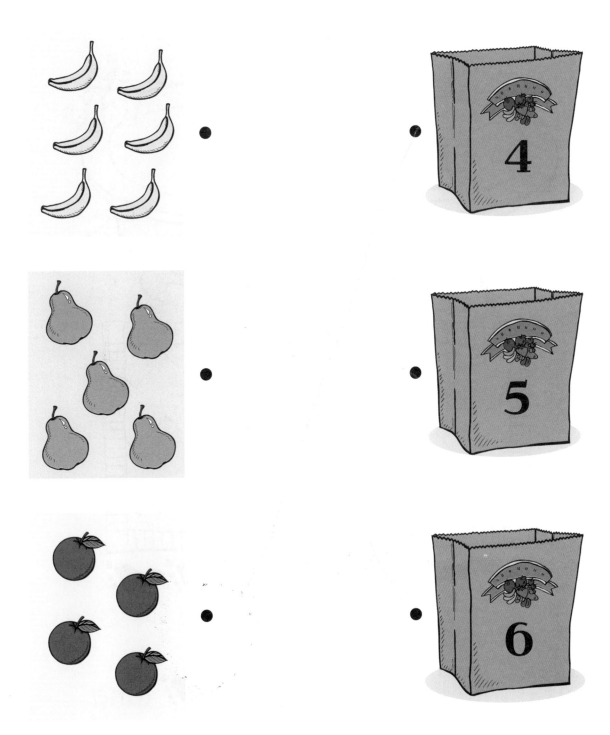

There is a mat on the floor. Count the  and write the correct number. Colour the mat.

The mat is about _____ 👣 long.

ISBN: 978-1-897457-86-3

Sam is going up to his bedroom. Write the missing numbers on the stairs.

Daniel saves his coins in the piggy banks. Count the coins and draw lines to match.

ISBN: 978-1-897457-86-3

Ada is picking apples in an orchard. Count and write how many apples there are in the basket.

There are _____ apples in the basket.

Daisy and Mary are playing and collecting shells on the beach. Colour the box with **8** shells.

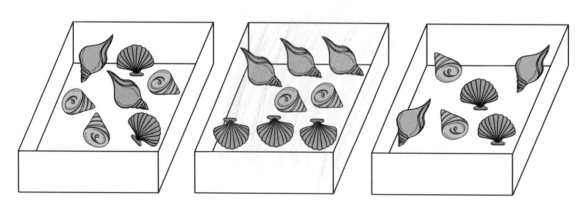

ISBN: 978-1-897457-86-3

The clown is tossing some balls. Draw more balls to make it **8**.

Math

The children have left their things on the field after the game. Count and circle the correct numbers.

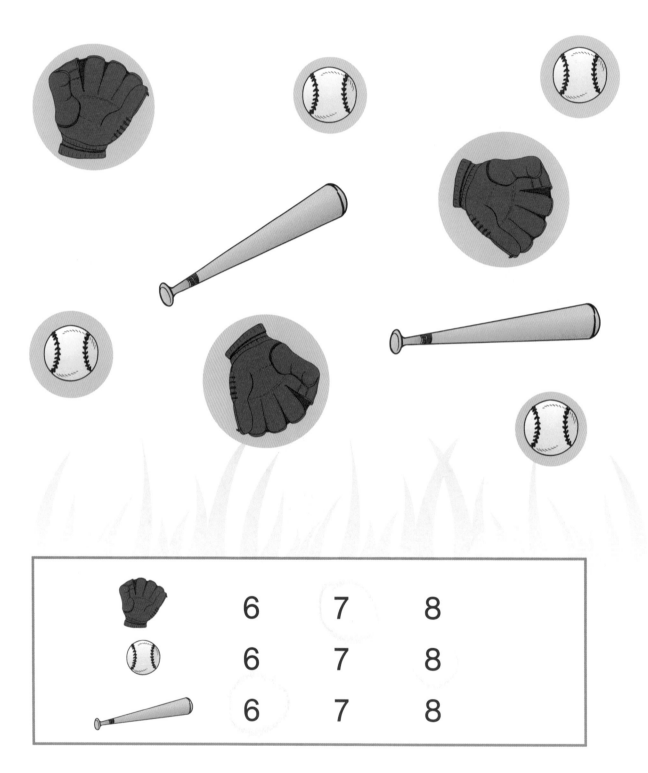

ISBN: 978-1-897457-86-3

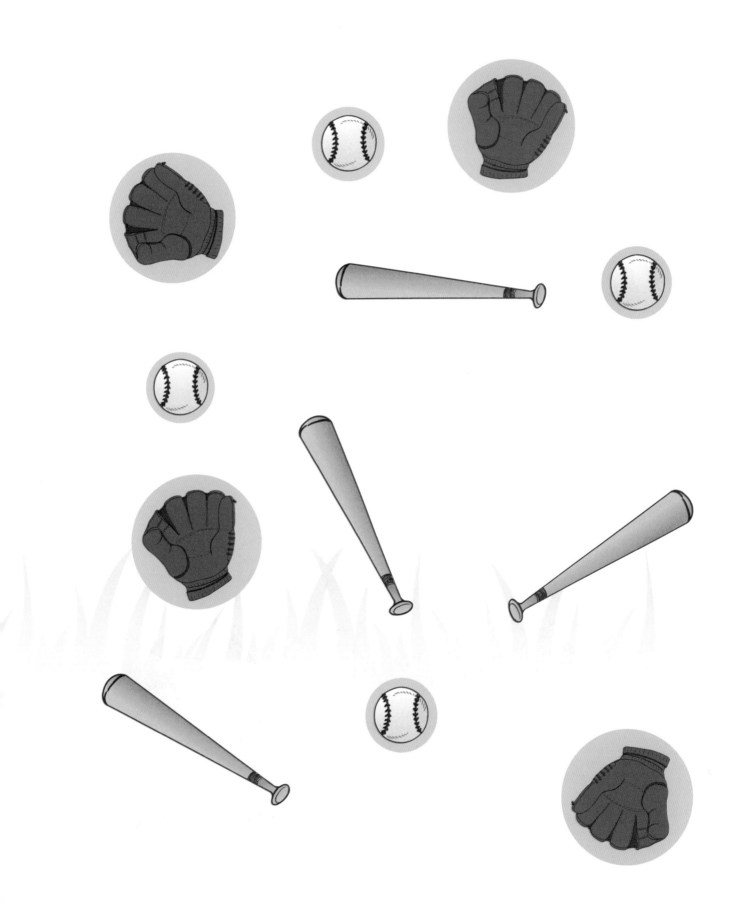

Help Jason find the way to buy a hot dog. Colour the path from **2 to 8**.

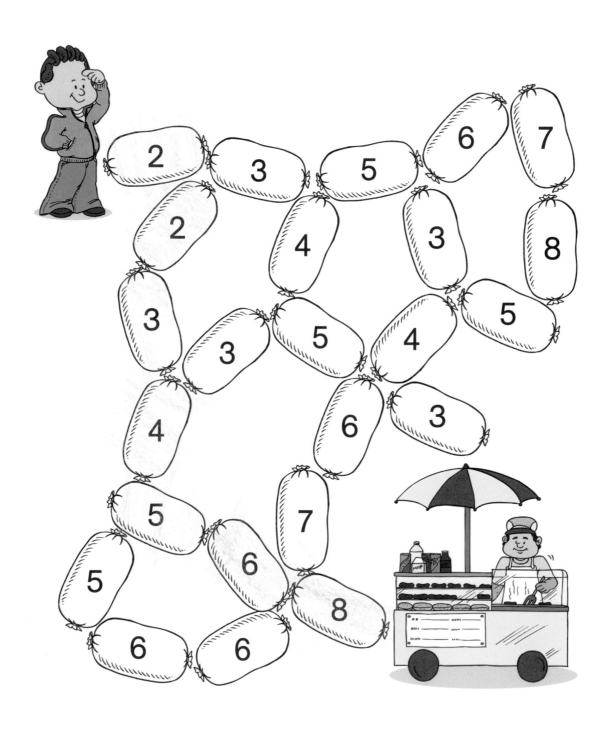

ISBN: 978-1-897457-86-3

Susan has drawn the smallest number. Which is Susan's prize? Colour it.

8

3

6

ISBN: 978-1-897457-86-3

The magician is taking some flowers out of his hat. Write the missing numbers.

ISBN: 978-1-897457-86-3

Mr. Smith has some sheep on his farm. Count and write how many sheep there are.

There are _____ sheep.

Look at Sam's phone. Write the missing numbers.

ISBN: 978-1-897457-86-3

Ricky and Jenny have collected many stickers. Put a ✔
to show who has more.

The children are reading on the carpet. How long is the carpet? Count the and write the correct number.

The carpet is about _____  long.

There are many toys in the toy shop. Count and circle the correct numbers.

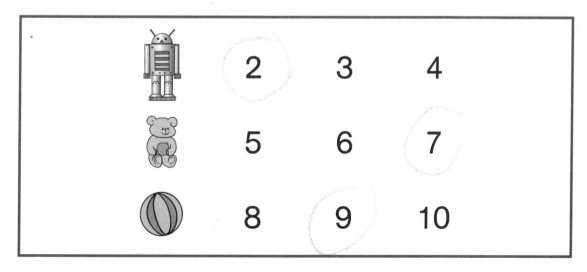

Help Kate put the candies into the right jars. Count and
draw lines to match.

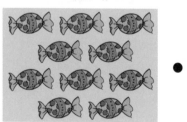

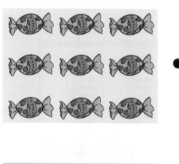

ISBN: 978-1-897457-86-3

The pets are lovely. Count and circle the correct numbers.

	2	3	4
	2	3	4

There are 8   9   10   pets in all.

There are many sailboats on the lake. Count and circle the correct number.

There are   8   9   10   sailboats on the lake.

ISBN: 978-1-897457-86-3

ISBN: 978-1-897457-86-3

It is time to get up. Write the missing numbers on the clock face.

ISBN: 978-1-897457-86-3

Janice always puts back her toys into the boxes after playing. Circle the correct answers.

Counting from the left:

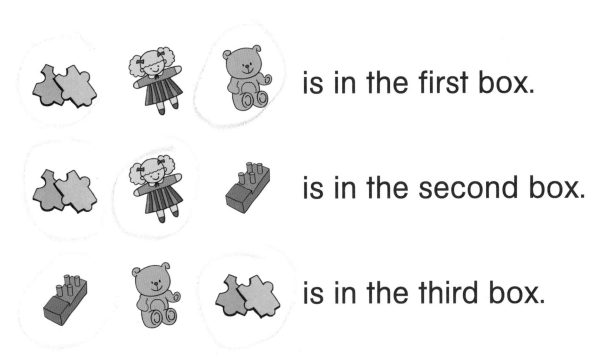

is in the first box.

is in the second box.

is in the third box.

ISBN: 978-1-897457-86-3

The children are lining up at the entrance. Circle the correct answers.

Who is first?

Who is second?

Who is third?

ISBN: 978-1-897457-86-3